Unashamed

Unashamed

by
John MacArthur, Jr.

MOODY PRESS
CHICAGO

All Scripture quotations, unless noted otherwise, are from the *New Ameri-
can Standard Bible*, © 1960, 1962, 1963, 1968, 1971, 1972, 1973, 1975, and
1977 by The Lockman Foundation, and are used by permission.

ISBN: 0-8024-5336-8

1 2 3 4 5 6 Printing/LC/Year 94 93 92 91 90

Printed in the United States of America

Contents

These Bible studies are taken from messages delivered by Pastor-Teacher John MacArthur, Jr., at Grace Community Church in Panorama City, California. The recorded messages themselves may be purchased as a series or individually. Please request the current price list by writing to:

"GRACE TO YOU"
P.O. Box 4000
Panorama City, CA 91412

Or call the following toll-free number:
1-800-55-GRACE

1
Motivating a Spiritual Son

Outline

Introduction
A. Paul's Greetings to Timothy
B. Paul's Circumstances in Rome
    1. Nero's plot
    2. Paul's plight
    3. God's plan
    4. Timothy's part
       a) His location
       b) His responsibilities
C. Paul's Instructions to Timothy
D. Paul's Concern for Timothy
    1. Timothy's struggles
       a) He might have been intimidated (2 Tim. 1:7)
       b) He might have been ashamed (2 Tim. 1:8)
       c) He might have been altering his theology (2 Tim. 1:13-14)
       d) He might have been neglecting his studies (2 Tim. 2:15)
       e) He might have been influenced by ungodly opinions (2 Tim. 2:16-17)
    2. Paul's exhortations
       a) Expect persecution (2 Tim. 3:1, 10-12, 14)
       b) Fulfill your ministry (2 Tim. 4:1-2)
       c) Be strong (2 Tim. 2:1)

Lesson

I. The Principle of Authority (vv. 1-2*a*)
   A. The Fact of Paul's Authority (vv. 1*a*, 2*a*)
      1. As stated by Paul
      2. As challenged by the critics
      3. As affirmed by the context
         a) A simple axiom
         b) A practical illustration
         c) A list of imperatives
   B. The Means of Paul's Authority (v. 1*b*)
   C. The Purpose of Paul's Authority (v. 1*c*)
II. The Principle of Altruism (v. 2*b*)
   A. Its Definition
   B. Its Manifestations
      1. Grace
      2. Mercy
      3. Peace
   C. Its Source
III. The Principle of Appreciation (v. 3*a-b*)
   A. Resulting in Thankful Prayers
   B. Coming from a Clear Conscience
      1. Paul's conscience
      2. Paul's forefathers
         a) A reference to Old Testament saints?
         b) A reference to Paul's own family?
         c) A reference to the other apostles?
         d) A reference to all believers?
IV. The Principle of Appeal (v. 3*c*)
   A. Its Emphasis
   B. Its Impact
V. The Principle of Affection (v. 4)
   A. Paul Longed for Timothy's Companionship
   B. Paul Remembered Timothy's Tears
   C. Paul Sought the Joy of Reunion
VI. The Principle of Affirmation (v. 5)
   A. Paul Affirmed the Genuineness of Timothy's Faith
   B. Paul Affirmed the Richness of Timothy's Faith

Conclusion

Introduction

When the apostle Paul wrote his second letter to Timothy, he knew his death was imminent and that Timothy would carry a heavy ministry responsibility in his absence. He therefore wrote Timothy to instruct and motivate him to fulfill his calling.

A. Paul's Greetings to Timothy

The letter begins, "Paul, an apostle of Christ Jesus by the will of God, according to the promise of life in Christ Jesus, to Timothy, my beloved son: Grace, mercy and peace from God the Father and Christ Jesus our Lord. I thank God, whom I serve with a clear conscience the way my forefathers did, as I constantly remember you in my prayers night and day, longing to see you, even as I recall your tears, so that I may be filled with joy. For I am mindful of the sincere faith within you, which first dwelt in your grandmother Lois, and your mother Eunice, and I am sure that it is in you as well" (vv. 1-5).

B. Paul's Circumstances in Rome

1. Nero's plot

In A.D. 64 the Roman Emperor Nero set fire to the city of Rome. To avoid public shame and wrath, he blamed it on the Christians. As a result, a wave of persecution aimed at Christians spread throughout the Roman Empire. Many Christians were imprisoned and executed.

2. Paul's plight

Because Paul was the leading spokesman for the Christian faith, he too was arrested. He was incarcerated in the Mamertine Prison in Rome, from whence he wrote 2 Timothy. His words reflect the gravity of the situation: "For I am already being poured out as a drink offering, and the time of my departure has come. I have fought the good fight, I have finished the course, I have kept the faith" (2 Tim. 4:6-7).

In a sense, 2 Timothy was Paul's final will and testament. As such we should study it with great care and a commitment to obey its teachings.

3. God's plan

Apparently Nero had sought to kill Paul prior to his final imprisonment, but Paul had been "delivered out of the lion's mouth" (2 Tim. 4:17). God graciously spared his life so that he might continue his ministry and write 2 Timothy.

4. Timothy's part

Of all the churches or individuals to whom Paul could have written at the end, he chose Timothy. Paul loved him deeply and knew he would be a key person in the propagation of the gospel after Paul's death. By way of 2 Timothy, Paul was passing the baton of leadership to Timothy.

a) His location

Timothy was probably in Ephesus when Paul wrote 2 Timothy. That is implied by the references to Ephesus in verse 18 of chapter 1 and verse 12 of chapter 4. Second Timothy 4:12 says, "Tychicus I have sent to Ephesus." The Greek construction of that sentence implies that Paul sent Tychicus to replace Timothy so the ministry at Ephesus would have competent leadership while Timothy visited Paul.

b) His responsibilities

When Paul wrote 2 Timothy, he was about sixty-six. He was nearing the end of his life and knew he would soon be with the Lord. But Timothy, who was about thirty-six, still faced the major responsibility of carrying the ministry into the next generation. In doing so he would have to face persecution and resistance to the truth without the support and companionship of Paul, his beloved spiritual father and mentor.

Do You Have a Sense of Mission?

A common characteristic of every great man of God is a sense of mission that extends beyond his own life. He is not driven by selfish ambition or the desires for success and personal comfort, but instead by a passion to do his part to contribute to the larger picture.

Paul was such a man. The continuation of the ministry was more important to him than the continuation of his own life. While imprisoned, he didn't feel sorry for himself or castigate the people who forsook him. His compelling desire was to build up godly men who could continue the ministry in his absence. That's why he solemnly charged Timothy to be faithful to his calling (2 Tim. 4:1).

Paul understood the importance of carrying on the work that Jesus began when He was on earth. Do you have a sense of mission? Remember, every Christian has an important part to play in spreading the gospel.

C. Paul's Instructions to Timothy

Second Timothy is Paul's list of instructions to Timothy about how he was to carry out the work of the ministry. The exhortations are clear, direct, and demanding; they call for the best effort Timothy—or any believer—has to offer.

D. Paul's Concern for Timothy

1. Timothy's struggles

Even though 2 Timothy is primarily instructional, beneath the surface it is actually an impassioned letter. Paul was deeply concerned, not only about the mission itself, but also about Timothy. He well knew Timothy's strengths and weaknesses, and there are hints throughout the epistle that Timothy was at a weak point in his life.

a) He might have been intimidated (2 Tim. 1:7)

"God has not given us a spirit of timidity, but of power and love and discipline."

"Timidity" suggests one who is cowardly, weak, and vacillating. Perhaps Timothy was weakening under the stress of dealing with ungodly leaders in the Ephesian church, a task Paul had assigned Timothy in his first letter. He might have felt intimidated because he couldn't answer all their arguments and objections to his teaching. But Paul reminded him of the power, love, and discipline that were his by God's grace. Therefore he didn't need to be intimidated by human resistance.

b) He might have been ashamed (2 Tim. 1:8)

"Do not be ashamed of the testimony of our Lord, or of me His prisoner; but join with me in suffering for the gospel according to the power of God."

Perhaps because of the growing persecution that was coming from Rome, Timothy was shying away from proclaiming Christ. Perhaps he thought that his identification with Paul, who was incarcerated as one of the leading Christian exponents, would threaten his own freedom or increase his suffering. Such fears might have led to subtle compromises in his ministry.

c) He might have been altering his theology (2 Tim. 1:13-14)

"Retain the standard of sound words which you have heard from me, in the faith and love which are in Christ Jesus. Guard, through the Holy Spirit who dwells in us, the treasure which has been entrusted to you."

Perhaps Timothy was tempted to alter his theology to avoid offending someone. Even the slightest drift toward weakness elicited serious concern from Paul.

d) He might have been neglecting his studies (2 Tim. 2:15)

"Be diligent to present yourself approved to God as a workman who does not need to be ashamed, handling accurately the word of truth."

Timothy was to be a disciplined student of God's truth so he could handle it accurately.

e) He might have been influenced by ungodly opinions (2 Tim. 2:16-17)

"Avoid worldly and empty chatter, for it will lead to further ungodliness, and their talk will spread like gangrene."

Perhaps Timothy was spending too much time listening to the false philosophies of his day and was becoming engulfed by them.

Other verses in chapter 2 imply that Timothy might have been struggling in other areas as well: "flee from youthful lusts, and pursue righteousness, faith, love and peace" (v. 22); "refuse foolish and ignorant speculations, knowing that they produce quarrels" (v. 23); "the Lord's bond-servant must not be quarrelsome, but be kind to all, able to teach, patient when wronged, with gentleness correcting those who are in opposition" (vv. 24-25).

Those statements might have been aimed at strengthening Timothy's spiritual character at a time when it was being weakened by severe persecution.

2. Paul's exhortations

Paul's exhortations to Timothy can be summarized in three statements:

a) Expect persecution (2 Tim. 3:1, 10-12, 14)

"Realize this, that in the last days difficult times will come. . . . You followed my . . . persecutions [and] sufferings, such as happened to me at Antioch, at Iconium and at Lystra. . . . Indeed, all who desire to live godly in Christ Jesus will be persecuted. . . . You, however, continue in the things you have learned and become convinced of, knowing from whom you have learned them."

b) Fulfill your ministry (2 Tim. 4:1-5)

"I solemnly charge you in the presence of God and of Christ Jesus, who is to judge the living and the dead, and by His appearing and His Kingdom: preach the Word. . . . Be sober in all things, endure hardship, do the work of an evangelist, fulfill your ministry."

c) Be strong (2 Tim. 2:1)

"My son, be strong in the grace that is in Christ Jesus."

Are You Passing the Baton?

Second Timothy presents an interesting contrast between Paul's strength and Timothy's struggles. It reflects most relationships where a mature believer is training a younger believer.

As a pastor, I understand the need to raise up other godly men who will carry on the ministry. Few works survive the death of the men who begin them, but the Christian ministry is different. It will continue until Jesus returns. In the meantime, all Christians should be involved in passing the baton of ministry to others (2 Tim. 2:2). Are you passing the baton?

Lesson

In 2 Timothy 1:1-5 we find applicable principles as we endeavor to motivate other believers toward spiritual growth and effective service.

I. THE PRINCIPLE OF AUTHORITY (vv. 1-2a)

A. The Fact of Paul's Authority (vv. 1a, 2a)

"Paul, an apostle of Christ Jesus . . . to Timothy, my beloved son."

As an apostle, Paul had spiritual authority over Timothy, and he understood that his authority was a key element in motivating Timothy to complete the ministry that had been entrusted to him.

The name *Paul* is synonymous with New Testament apostolic authority. Paul was his Greek name. It means "little." Saul was his Hebrew name. He probably used both names all his life, since he was of the Jewish tribe of Benjamin yet lived in a Greek culture. In Scripture he is called Saul until Acts 13:9, when he began his ministry to the Gentiles. From then on he is called Paul.

1. As stated by Paul

Paul identified himself as "an apostle of Christ Jesus" (v. 1). The Greek word translated "apostle" means "a sent one, emissary, ambassador, or envoy." His authority was grounded in the fact that he was called by Jesus Himself to be an apostle.

Shortly after Paul's conversion on the Damascus road (Acts 9:3-6), the Lord appeared in a vision to a disciple named Ananias, saying, "[Paul] is a chosen instrument of Mine, to bear My name before the Gentiles and kings and the sons of Israel; for I will show him how much he must suffer for My name's sake" (Acts 9:15-16).

When Paul defends his ministry in Acts 22 and 26, he reiterates that the Lord has chosen him as a representative in proclaiming the gospel of Jesus Christ.

2. As challenged by the critics

Some critics of Scripture deny the Pauline authorship of 2 Timothy on the assumption that Paul would not begin a tender, loving letter to Timothy with technical data about his apostleship. They claim that as Paul's loving child in the faith and companion in ministry, Timothy would not need verification of his authority.

3. As affirmed by the context

   a) A simple axiom

      However, that viewpoint reflects a failure to understand the simple axiom that intimacy never precludes authority. For example, how could a father properly train his children if he attempted to do so on the basis of love apart from his authority? How could a boss properly supervise his or her employees on the basis of friendship without authority? It wouldn't work! Love and friendship must never preclude authority.

   b) A practical illustration

      Paul affirmed his authority, but he didn't stop there. In 2 Timothy 1:2 he says, "To Timothy, my beloved son." That expression of intimacy gives balance to his assertion of authority.

      There was a deep love and spiritual bond between Paul and Timothy, but Paul was still in authority over him and was the one through whom God communicated His Word to Timothy.

   c) A list of imperatives

      The many imperatives Paul gives throughout 2 Timothy presuppose his authority:

      (1) "Kindle afresh the gift of God which is in you" (1:6).

      (2) "Do not be ashamed of the testimony of our Lord, or of me" (1:8).

      (3) "Retain the standard of sound words" (1:13).

      (4) "Guard . . . the treasure which has been entrusted to you" (1:14).

(5) "Be strong in the grace that is in Christ Jesus" (2:1).

(6) "The things which you have heard from me . . . entrust to faithful men" (2:2).

(7) "Suffer hardship with me" (2:3).

(8) "Remember Jesus Christ" (2:8).

(9) "Remind them of these things, and solemnly charge them" (2:14).

(10) "Be diligent" (2:15).

(11) "Avoid worldly and empty chatter" (2:16).

(12) "Flee from youthful lusts, and pursue righteousness, faith, love and peace" (2:22).

(13) "Refuse foolish and ignorant speculations" (2:23).

(14) "Continue in the things you have learned" (3:14).

(15) "Preach the word; be ready . . . reprove, rebuke, exhort" (4:2).

(16) "Be sober in all things, endure hardship, do the work of an evangelist, fulfill your ministry" (4:5).

When Paul spoke for God, he did so with divine authority. Although we don't receive direct revelation as Paul did, when we communicate God's Word in a discipling relationship, we too speak with divine authority. We may develop close friendships and share sweet fellowship with those whom we disciple, but we must never relinquish our authority because it is based on the fact that we speak from God's Word.

B. The Means of Paul's Authority (v. 1*b*)

"By the will of God."

Paul was an apostle of Jesus Christ because God willed it to be so. The Greek word translated "will" (*thelēma*) means a deep desire. It was God's deep desire that Paul be sent by Christ.

By sovereignly choosing Paul, God placed him under divine orders to preach the gospel. Consequently, when Paul instructed Timothy to change his behavior or to stand firm in his ministry, he was not simply making suggestions. He was giving authoritative commandments from God Himself.

C. The Purpose of Paul's Authority (v. 1c)

"According to the promise of life in Christ Jesus."

Paul was granted divine authority so that he might preach about eternal life in Christ. "In Christ Jesus" is a favorite Pauline phrase that speaks of the union with Christ that salvation brings—we become one with Him in His death, resurrection, and new life.

Jesus said, "I came that they might have life, and might have it abundantly" (John 10:10). He also said, "I am the way, the truth, and the life" (John 14:6). John 3:16 says, "God so loved the world, that He gave His only begotten Son, that whosoever believes in Him should not perish, but have eternal life."

God commissioned Paul to preach the gospel of eternal life in Christ Jesus. Therefore he was under divine authority.

II. THE PRINCIPLE OF ALTRUISM (v. 2b)

"Grace, mercy and peace from God the Father and Christ Jesus our Lord."

A. Its Definition

Altruism is unselfish concern for the welfare of others. Paul expressed such a concern for Timothy in wishing him God's grace, mercy, and peace.

B. Its Manifestations

1. Grace

Grace is God's undeserved favor, including His love and forgiveness. It frees sinners from bondage to sin and enables them to serve God.

2. Mercy

Mercy is God's undeserved compassion as He frees sinners from the misery created by their sin.

3. Peace

Peace is the tranquillity of heart that results from being in a right relationship with God. It is the direct result of His grace and mercy.

Paul desired God's best for Timothy: grace to cover his sins, mercy to overrule his misery, and peace to dominate his life.

C. Its Source

Grace, mercy, and peace come from "God the Father and Christ Jesus our Lord" (v. 2). Paul equated the Father and the Son as the source of grace, mercy, and peace, thereby equating their deity as well.

In seeking God's best for Timothy, Paul demonstrated his altruistic spirit. We too must show our disciples that their spiritual well-being is of utmost concern to us. That can be a source of great encouragement and motivation to them. Even though they are under our authority, we must demonstrate to them our kindness.

III. THE PRINCIPLE OF APPRECIATION (v. 3a-b)

"I thank God, whom I serve with a clear conscience the way my forefathers did, as I constantly remember you."

A. Resulting in Thankful Prayers

Even though Paul was incarcerated in a crowded, filthy dungeon and faced an unjust execution, he wasn't angry, bitter, or vengeful. Instead, he was constantly thinking about Timothy, praying for him, and longing to see him again.

In verse 3 the emphasis in the Greek text is on Paul's thankfulness. Paul didn't know if he would see Timothy again, but he was deeply grateful to God for him.

He thanked God rather than Timothy because he knew that anything Timothy had accomplished had been done only by God's grace. After all, it was God who had sovereignly saved, called, gifted, and appointed Timothy to the ministry.

B. Coming from a Clear Conscience

1. Paul's conscience

Paul served God with a clear conscience. He knew that his impending death was not the result of any sin on his part. The Greek word translated "serve" (*latreuō*) refers to temple service and could be translated "worship."

Paul may have mentioned his clear conscience in an effort to silence anyone who might have thought he was in prison because God was chastening him. Some had apparently come to that conclusion about his first imprisonment (Phil. 1:12-20).

First Timothy 1:5 says, "The goal of our instruction is love from a pure heart and a good conscience and a sincere faith." In 1 Timothy 3:9 Paul exhorts Timothy to hold "to the mystery of the faith with a clear conscience." First Timothy 4:2 speaks of "the hypocrisy of liars seared in their own conscience as with a branding iron" because they constantly reject the truth.

Paul carefully guarded his conscience, and it didn't condemn him for being in prison. He knew that his imprisonment was by the sovereign hand of God for His own glory.

2. Paul's forefathers

Paul was confident that he served God in the same way his forefathers had. We can't know for sure to whom "forefathers" refers, but there are four possibilities:

a) A reference to Old Testament saints?

Some expositors think Paul was referring to Old Testament saints like Abraham, Isaac, Jacob, Joseph, Moses, Isaiah, Daniel, Jeremiah, and Ezekiel—Paul's Jewish forefathers.

b) A reference to Paul's own family?

In Philippians 3:5 Paul states that he was "circumcised the eighth day, of the nation of Israel, of the tribe of Benjamin, a Hebrew of Hebrews; as to the Law, a Pharisee." He might have had his devout Jewish family in mind.

c) A reference to the other apostles?

Peter, James, John, Philip, Nathaniel, Bartholomew, and the other apostles were Paul's spiritual forefathers.

d) A reference to all believers?

Since Paul didn't specifically say whom he had in mind, it seems best to assume he meant all who had faithfully served God before him—whether Old or New Testament saints.

If that's the case, Paul was saying he had served the Lord with a clear conscience, just as all those who had faithfully served Him in the past. Of course many of them had been unjustly accused, imprisoned, and put to death. So anyone who claimed that Paul's imprisonment was a result of his sin needed to check back through Scripture to see how others suffered for righteousness' sake (cf. Heb. 11).

Do You Appreciate Those Who Minister to You?

Quite often the closer we are to a person the more prone we are to take him or her for granted. But that wasn't the case with Paul and Timothy. Paul knew Timothy very well. He had traveled with him, shared meals with him, and observed him in many struggles and trials of life. He knew his strengths and weaknesses. Yet when Paul faced the greatest trial of his life, his great appreciation for Timothy was on his mind. And he took time to let Timothy know that. Such encouragement goes a long way to motivate someone who is struggling with the ongoing responsibilities of life and ministry.

I can imagine the impact Paul's appreciation must have had on Timothy. In the early years of my ministry, men of God whom I greatly respected told me that they appreciated my ministry and were praying for me. Their confidence placed a heavy weight of responsibility on my shoulders, but it also served as a great source of motivation and encouragement. I am deeply indebted to them.

Be careful never to take for granted those who minister to you. Pray for them and express your gratitude to them often!

IV. THE PRINCIPLE OF APPEAL (v. 3c)

"As I constantly remember you in my prayers night and day."

A. Its Emphasis

It might seem redundant for Paul to say that he prayed "constantly . . . night and day." Apparently he wanted to emphasize the consistency of his prayers for Timothy. The Greek word translated "constantly" means uninterrupted, unceasing prayer. We find it in 1 Thessalonians 5:17: "Pray without ceasing." The Greek word translated "prayer" (deēsis) means "to petition or plead to God on behalf of others."

Perhaps day and night were indistinguishable to Paul in the darkness of the Mamertine Prison, but his meaning is clear: he constantly thought of Timothy and prayed for him. He also prayed unceasingly for the Roman church (Rom. 1:9-10), the Corinthian church (1 Cor. 1:4), the Philippian church (Phil. 1:3-4), the Colossian church (Col. 1:3), the Thessalonian church (1 Thess. 1:2), and for his friend Philemon (Philem. 1:4). Prayer was a way of life for Paul.

B. Its Impact

It is compelling for a disciple to know that his mentor is constantly praying for him. It also gives him the assurance that God's power is at work on his behalf because "the effective prayer of a righteous man can accomplish much" (James 5:16). Surely Paul's faithful prayers greatly impacted Timothy.

If you want to motivate someone to excel in his spiritual life and ministry, put him under your authority, demonstrate that you have his best interests at heart, and remind him often how much you appreciate and pray for him.

V. THE PRINCIPLE OF AFFECTION (v. 4)

"Longing to see you, even as I recall your tears, so that I may be filled with joy."

A. Paul Longed for Timothy's Companionship

Paul greatly missed Timothy and wanted him to make every effort to come to Rome before winter set in (2 Tim. 4:9, 21). The Greek word translated "longing" (*epipotheō*) means "to have a strong desire" or "yearning." Paul's heart was aching to see Timothy again.

B. Paul Remembered Timothy's Tears

Apparently Timothy wept the last time he and Paul parted company. We don't know when that was, but it's likely that Paul visited Timothy at Ephesus some time after he wrote 1 Timothy and before his final arrest. Their deep love for each other made it a tearful parting—similar to the touching account of Paul's farewell to the Ephesian elders.

The elders wept out loud, embraced him, and repeatedly kissed him (Acts 20:37).

The years of ministry, fellowship, travel, danger, and suffering that Paul and Timothy shared had knit their hearts closely together. The thought of Timothy's tears undoubtedly made Paul all the more anxious to see him.

C. Paul Sought the Joy of Reunion

Separation from Timothy had caused Paul sadness; seeing Timothy again would fill him with joy. That's how much Paul loved his beloved son in the faith.

Such expressions of love are great motivators. If you want to nurture someone in the faith, tell that person how deeply you love him or her. Who can resist the compulsion of love?

VI. THE PRINCIPLE OF AFFIRMATION (v. 5)

"I am mindful of the sincere faith within you, which first dwelt in your grandmother Lois, and your mother Eunice, and I am sure that it is in you as well."

Even though Timothy seems to have been struggling, Paul expressed confidence in the genuineness and richness of his faith. He knew Timothy had the spiritual substance to overcome his weaknesses and to fulfill his ministry. Paul didn't say, "Oh Timothy, you really disappoint me. What a weak, wishy-washy character you are. It's questionable whether you'll ever survive!" Rather than planting doubts in his mind, Paul affirmed Timothy.

A. Paul Affirmed the Genuineness of Timothy's Faith

"I am mindful" is a passive action. Somehow Paul had received a reminder of Timothy's genuine faith. We don't know how it happened—perhaps it was just his prayers or his memories. Maybe it was a letter or a note from Timothy or someone who had met him.

The Greek word translated "sincere" (*anupokritos*) means "without hypocrisy or phoniness." It speaks of something that is genuine. Timothy was a "true child in the faith" (1 Tim. 1:2); his faith was genuine.

B. Paul Affirmed the Richness of Timothy's Faith

Timothy's faith was rich because he was the product of a godly family. It is probable that Paul knew of the faith of Timothy's mother and grandmother because he and Barnabas led them to Christ during their visit to Galatia on the first missionary journey (Acts 14:6-7). Eunice and Lois were devout Jewish women who loved God and responded to the gospel.

Timothy had a Gentile father (Acts 16:1), who probably died sometime prior to Paul's first missionary journey. By the time Paul returned to Galatia on his second missionary journey (Acts 16:1-3), Lois and Eunice had evidently led young Timothy to Christ. He was therefore the recipient of the rich spiritual heritage of his mother and grandmother and was indirectly a spiritual child of Paul (2 Tim. 1:2).

Paul said of Timothy, "From childhood you have known the sacred writings which are able to give you the wisdom that leads to salvation through faith which is in Christ Jesus" (2 Tim. 3:15). That was the foundational aspect of his spiritual heritage.

The Value of a Godly Heritage

Recently I met with other Christian leaders to consider some candidates for a significant ministry position. During our deliberations I noticed that the father of each of the candidates was a prominent pastor. Each candidate had grown up in a family that taught him biblical truth and exemplified it in their daily living.

The candidates had not been chosen on that basis, but their heritage was so rich that it had obviously impacted their lives. Consequently they stood out above their peers as uniquely qualified for such a ministry position.

That's a tremendous commentary on the richness and depth that a Christian heritage adds to a spiritual leader. And Timothy was the beneficiary of such a heritage—first through his mother and grand-mother, then through Paul himself.

Conclusion

I believe everyone in spiritual leadership should know these six principles of motivation so that they can properly disciple those who are less mature in the faith: *authority* (disciples need to know they are accountable to obey God's Word), *altruism* (you have their best interests at heart), *appreciation* (you are thankful to God for them), *appeal* (you constantly pray for them), *affection* (you have a deep, loving relationship with them), and *affirmation* (you express your confidence in their ability to succeed spiritually).

All these principles are so universal that they could be applied beyond the discipling process to any area of life. But our primary task is to make disciples (Matt. 28:19) and motivate them to minister effectively for the Lord. As we apply each principle in the discipling process, we'll have a major impact on those whom God has placed in our care.

Focusing on the Facts

1. Who set fire to Rome? Who was blamed (see p. 9)?
2. What was the name of the prison in which Paul was incarcerated when he wrote 2 Timothy (see p. 9)?
3. In a sense, 2 Timothy was Paul's final _____ and _____ (see p. 10).
4. What indications do we have that Timothy was at Ephesus when he received 2 Timothy (see p. 10)?
5. Approximately how old was Paul when he wrote 2 Timothy (see p. 10)?
6. What characterizes a man with a sense of mission (see p. 11)?
7. List five areas of ministry in which Timothy was apparently struggling (see pp. 12-13).
8. What are three exhortations that Paul gave to Timothy (see pp. 13-14)?
9. Second Timothy presents an interesting contrast between Paul's _____ and Timothy's _____ (see p. 14).
10. Define "apostle" (see p. 15).

11. On what basis do some critics deny the Pauline authorship of 2 Timothy (see pp. 15-16)?
12. Intimacy never precludes _____ (see p. 16).
13. What was the means of Paul's authority (2 Tim. 1:1; see pp. 17-18)?
14. What was the purpose of Paul's authority (2 Tim. 1:1; see p. 18)?
15. What is altruism, and how does it figure into 2 Timothy 1:2 (see p. 18)?
16. Describe "grace," "mercy," and "peace" as used in 2 Timothy 1:2 (see p. 19).
17. Why did Paul say that he "served God with a clear conscience" (2 Tim. 1:3; see p. 20)?
18. What are four options for Paul's use of "forefathers" in 2 Timothy 1:3? Which option is probably best? Why (see pp. 21-22)?
19. What did Paul mean when he said he prayed for Timothy "constantly . . . night and day" (2 Tim. 1:3; see pp. 22-23)?
20. Define "sincere" as used in 2 Timothy 1:5 (see pp. 24-25).

Pondering the Principles

1. We have seen that a common characteristic of all great men of God is a sense of mission that extends beyond his own life and compels him to spend his life contributing all he can to the advancement of God's kingdom. That includes training others to carry on the ministry in his absence. Although that sense of mission is common to such men, it must never be limited to them. Every believer plays a vital role in passing on the gospel to the next generation. In that sense every day of your life has eternal significance. Pray that God will help you use each one wisely. And be sure to share with others the things He is teaching you from His Word.

2. God was gracious in using Paul to encourage and motivate Timothy during a very difficult time in Timothy's life. We too have times of struggle, but we may not always have someone like Paul to help us along the way. At such times it's crucial that we draw strength and encouragement from prayer and the ministry of God's Word. Remember, Christ is in authority over us (Matt. 28:18), but He always has our best interest at heart (Rom. 8:28; 1 Cor. 10:13), loves and appreciates us with a pure love

(1 John 3:1), continually appeals to the Father on our behalf (Rom. 8:26-28; Heb. 7:25), and knows that ultimately we will succeed (Phil. 1:6; Jude 24). What wonderful promises, and what a rich source of spiritual motivation!

2
Not Being Ashamed of Christ—Part 1

Outline

Introduction
A. Paul's Circumstances
B. Timothy's Character
C. Timothy's Circumstances

Review

Lesson
A. The Definition of Not Being Ashamed of Christ
B. The Reasons Christians Sometimes Are Ashamed of Christ
C. The Consequences of Being Ashamed of Christ
   1. It stifles our service
     a) Peter's denial of Christ
     b) Christ's restoration of Peter
   2. It betrays our beliefs
     a) Being ashamed of Christ is characteristic of unbelievers
     b) Being ashamed of Christ is uncharacteristic of believers
   3. It perverts our perspective
     a) Jesus is not ashamed of us
     b) God is not ashamed of us
I. Renew Your Gift (v. 6)
A. The Rationale (v. 6*a*)
B. The Response (v. 6*b*)
C. The Resource (v. 6*c*)
D. The Reception (v. 6*d*)

Conclusion

Introduction

A. Paul's Circumstances

In 2 Timothy 1:6-18 the apostle Paul addresses the issue of not being ashamed of Christ. When he wrote 2 Timothy he was incarcerated in a Roman prison and knew that his life was about to end. In Paul's absence Timothy would be largely responsible for advancing the gospel and developing qualified spiritual leadership for the church. Paul encouraged him to "be strong in the grace that is in Christ Jesus" (2 Tim. 2:1). The entire epistle echoes the theme of spiritual strength amidst severe opposition.

Paul was obviously concerned about Timothy's personal well-being, but his compelling goal was to motivate Timothy to carry on the work of the ministry. Even as he languished in prison with only Luke to minister to him (2 Tim. 4:11), Paul never lost sight of the priority of advancing Christ's kingdom.

B. Timothy's Character

Apparently Timothy was not as indomitable as Paul, who was a forceful, dynamic personality and who stood unwaveringly for the cause of Christ against many opponents. Timothy, on the other hand, probably drew much of his strength from Paul, and Paul knew that Timothy needed to learn to rely more heavily on the Holy Spirit's power (2 Tim. 1:6-7).

In addition to the glimpses of Timothy's character that we see in 2 Timothy, 1 Corinthians 16:10 adds this insight: "If Timothy comes, see that he is with you without cause to be afraid; for he is doing the Lord's work." Perhaps Timothy was intimidated or fearful when circumstances were against him. Even so, he had a significant ministry wherever he went, and it was crucial that he learn to persevere despite opposition.

C. Timothy's Circumstances

Timothy was a relatively young man (probably in his mid to late thirties) ministering at Ephesus when he received 2 Timothy. His ministry wasn't easy. According to 1 Timothy, he had to confront people in the highest levels of church leadership and defend himself against the prevailing philosophical and theological views of his day. In addition, the Romans had unleashed wholehearted persecution against all Christians, whom they falsely blamed for the burning of Rome.

With such severe opposition, Timothy was in danger of being arrested and executed for preaching Christ. But he was Paul's protégé, and much time, effort, and prayer had been invested in his training. It was therefore vital that he not waver under pressure and that he fulfill his ministry for the sake of the next generation of Christians who would be the recipients of God's grace through him.

Review

At the beginning of Paul's second letter to Timothy we see five principles that motivate the believer to persevere in the midst of opposition: the principles of authority (vv. 1-2*a*; see pp. 15-18), altruism (v. 2*b*; see pp. 18-19), appreciation (v. 3*a-b*; see pp. 19-22), appeal (v. 3*c*; see pp. 22-23), affection (v. 4; see pp. 23-24), and affirmation (v. 5; see pp. 24-26).

Lesson

After motivating Timothy, Paul exhorted him not to be ashamed of Christ (vv. 6-18).

A. The Definition of Not Being Ashamed of Christ

Not being ashamed of Christ is having the courage and boldness to speak for Christ at every opportunity, no matter what the cost might be.

B. The Reasons Christians Sometimes Are Ashamed of Christ

All of us have occasions when we are afraid to speak of Christ or be identified with Him. In some cases it's the result of severe persecution such as Timothy was facing. But most often it is simply because "the fear of man brings a snare" (Prov. 29:25). We fear what others might say about us or how they will react to us if we're outspoken about Christ.

Sometimes we're embarrassed or afraid we won't have the right words to say. At other times the sin in our lives leads us to be silent out of fear that someone will confront our hypocrisy. In some cases our job or reputation will be jeopardized if we identify with Christ. But if we are going to be successful in serving the Lord, we have to conquer our fear and our shame.

C. The Consequences of Being Ashamed of Christ

1. It stifles our service

    a) Peter's denial of Christ

    Peter is the classic example of someone who was ashamed of Christ. When Jesus was arrested (Matthew 26), His disciples left Him and fled (v. 56). However, Peter followed at a distance to see what would happen to his Master (v. 58). As he was sitting in a courtyard outside the place where Jesus was being interrogated, "a certain servant girl came to him and said, 'You . . . were with Jesus the Galilean.' But he denied it before them all, saying, 'I do not know what you are talking about' " (vv. 69-70). Peter lied, rather than place his life in jeopardy by identifying himself with Jesus.

    Verses 71-75 say, "When he had gone out to the gateway, another servant girl saw him and said to those who were there, 'This man was with Jesus of Nazareth.' And again he denied it with an oath, 'I do not know the man.' And a little later the bystanders came up and said to Peter, 'Surely you too are one of them; for the way you talk gives you away.' Then he began to curse and swear, 'I do not know the man!'

And immediately a cock crowed. And Peter remembered the word which Jesus had said, 'Before a cock crows, you will deny Me three times.' And he went out and wept bitterly."

Peter was clearly ashamed of Christ, and most of us would agree that he acted in a deceitful, weak, unthankful, and unloving manner toward Jesus. Yet there are times when all of us fail to speak for Christ. We may not do it the same way Peter did, but we are ashamed nonetheless.

Even Timothy struggled with fear and intimidation. I don't think he had grown completely cold in his spiritual life, but the fire was perhaps waning a bit. Apparently the battles he faced were taking a toll on him because 2 Timothy contains very little commendation. It is mostly a series of exhortations.

b) Christ's restoration of Peter

Even after such a serious denial of Christ, Peter was forgiven and restored to ministry. That should encourage us when we fail and are in need of His forgiveness.

Peter's restoration occurred when he and Jesus met on the shore of the Sea of Galilee (John 21:1) sometime after Jesus' resurrection. Peter had denied Him three times, so Jesus gave him three opportunities to affirm his love, which he did without hesitation (vv. 15-17). When Peter was ashamed of Christ, he was useless for ministry. But after his restoration, he was once again useful. So Jesus commanded him three times to tend His lambs and shepherd His sheep, which was a metaphorical way of saying, "Nurture My people."

Jesus knew that Peter's love was genuine and that he would even stand the test of martyrdom. In verses 18-19 He says, " 'Truly, truly, I say to you, when you were younger, you used to gird yourself, and walk wherever you wished; but when you grow old, you will stretch out your hands, and someone else will gird you, and bring you where you do not wish to go.' Now this He said, signifying by what kind of death [Peter] would glorify God."

From that day forward, Peter followed Jesus. And on the Day of Pentecost he stood up in Jerusalem and with great boldness, courage, and conviction denounced the Jewish people for crucifying the One whom God had made both Lord and Christ (Acts 2:36). He preached about the resurrection of Christ and the judgment of God so powerfully that the people cried out, saying, " 'What shall we do?' And Peter said to them, 'Repent, and let each of you be baptized in the name of Jesus Christ' " (vv. 37-38). Approximately three thousand people were converted that day (v. 41).

Peter went from being ashamed of Christ to being a bold proclaimer of the gospel. Not only did he preach with power on the Day of Pentecost, but also we learn that he filled all Jerusalem with Christ's teaching (Acts 5:28).

When he was dragged before the Jewish religious leaders and commanded to stop preaching, he said, "Whether it is right in the sight of God to give heed to you rather than to God, you be the judge; for we cannot stop speaking what we have seen and heard" (Acts 4:19-20). And he thanked God that he had been considered worthy to suffer shame for Christ's sake (Acts 5:41).

2. It betrays our beliefs

   a) Being ashamed of Christ is characteristic of unbelievers

      (1) Matthew 10:32-39—Jesus said, "Everyone . . . who shall confess Me before men, I will also confess him before My Father who is in heaven. But whoever shall deny Me before men, I will also deny him before My Father who is in heaven" (vv. 32-33).

      Those verses show the relationship of confession to salvation. If you won't acknowledge Christ as your Lord, He won't acknowledge you as His child.

34

Jesus knew there was a high price to pay in Jewish culture for identifying with Him. Such a choice led to alienation from one's family and friends. That's why He said, "Do not think that I came to bring peace on the earth. . . . For I came to set a man against his father, and a daughter against her mother, and a daughter-in-law against her mother-in-law; and a man's enemies will be the members of his household" (v. 34).

The issue is love. Do you love Jesus more than whatever is most dear to you—your own family or your own life? Jesus went on to say, "He who loves father or mother more than Me is not worthy of Me; and he who loves son or daughter more than Me is not worthy of Me. And he who does not take his cross and follow after Me [is not willing to die for Me] is not worthy of Me. He who has found his life shall lose it, and he who has lost his life for My sake shall find it" (vv. 37-39).

If you are willing to profess your faith in Christ even if doing so may bring family rejection or death, He will claim you as His own before the Father. But if you constantly deny Him and are ashamed of Him, He will deny you.

(2) Mark 8:36-38—Jesus said, "What does it profit a man to gain the whole world, and forfeit his soul? For what shall a man give in exchange for his soul? For whoever is ashamed of Me and My words in this adulterous and sinful generation, the Son of Man will also be ashamed of him when He comes in the glory of His Father with the holy angels" (cf. Luke 9:25-26).

Those passages tell us that being ashamed of Christ is characteristic of unbelievers. Those who ultimately deny Christ will be denied by Him and will be consigned to eternal hell. He will not allow anyone into His presence who doesn't confess Him.

b) Being ashamed of Christ is uncharacteristic of believers

A believer who is ashamed of Christ acts like an unbeliever. The very title "Christian" implies that we are like Christ. That's our identity. We live to exalt His name, not deny it. But sadly, we do deny Him from time to time—just as we occasionally indulge in other sins. But such behavior is inconsistent with who we are in Christ. The Holy Spirit therefore convicts us to repent and turn from our sins. All true believers will do so.

3. It perverts our perspective

a) Jesus is not ashamed of us

Hebrews 2:10-12 says, "It was fitting for Him, for whom are all things, and through whom are all things, in bringing many sons to glory, to perfect the author of their salvation through sufferings. For both He [Christ] who sanctifies and those who are sanctified [believers] are all from one Father; for which reason He is not ashamed to call them brethren, saying, 'I will proclaim Thy name to My brethren.' "

Frankly, Jesus has every reason to be ashamed of us because we fail Him so often and bring dishonor to His name. Yet still He calls us brothers. How can we, who are so sinful, ever be ashamed of the One who is sinless?

b) God is not ashamed of us

Hebrews 11:16 says that Abraham and his descendants desired "a better country, that is a heavenly one. Therefore God is not ashamed to be called their God; for He has prepared a city for them." Those Old Testament saints lived by faith and willingly put their lives on the line because their eyes were focused on heaven rather than on the earth. God is not ashamed to be called the God of anyone who belongs to Him and lives for His glory.

It's a serious thing to be ashamed of Christ. It stifles our service, betrays our beliefs, and perverts our perspective.

We have seen some of the consequences of being ashamed of Christ, but how can we avoid falling into that sin? Paul's exhortation in 2 Timothy 1:6-18 suggests eight ways that we can live a life of boldness and confidence.

I. RENEW YOUR GIFT (v. 6)

"For this reason I remind you to kindle afresh the gift of God which is in you through the laying on of my hands."

Paul was exhorting Timothy to focus on the reason for his existence. That is the first step in cultivating boldness. As Christians, we were redeemed by God to proclaim the name of Christ and gifted by the Spirit to live for His glory. Therefore, being ashamed of Christ strikes a blow at the root of our being and cripples our effectiveness.

Like Timothy, we sometimes need to renew our commitment to use the gifts we've been given. If we neglect our spiritual responsibilities, we have lost sight of our purpose.

A. The Rationale (v. 6a)

"For this reason I remind you."

We find the reason for Paul's reminder in verse 5: "I am mindful of the sincere faith within you, which first dwelt in your grandmother Lois, and your mother Eunice, and I am sure that it is in you as well." Paul knew that Timothy's faith was genuine and that it had come to him by way of his mother and grandmother. In effect he was saying, "Because I know you're a true believer and I know your spiritual heritage, I therefore know you have a gift from God and you need to use it."

That's true of every believer. We've all been gifted spiritually. First Corinthians 12:11 says that the Holy Spirit distributes spiritual gifts to every believer according to His sovereign will. Romans 12 says that every believer has been gifted consistent with the measure of faith and grace given to him (vv. 3-6). So whatever your gifts are, be faithful to use them. That's what you are here for!

B. The Response (v. 6*b*)

"Kindle afresh."

Paul's use of the Greek present infinitive indicates the ongoing response he desired from Timothy. Kindling afresh his spiritual gift was to be continuous, rather than a one-time action. Paul expresses a similar idea in 1 Corinthians 15:31, where he says, "I die daily." He didn't worry about himself, try to protect himself, or bring comfort to himself. His daily goal was to exalt Christ no matter what the personal cost might be. That's what he wanted Timothy to do as well.

C. The Resource (v. 6*c*)

"The gift of God which is in you."

The Greek word translated "gift" (*charisma*) means "a gift of grace" or "grace gift." You don't earn it, gain it, seek it, or deserve it. The Holy Spirit gives every believer the gift or gifts that His sovereign will determines to be best suited for that individual and the proper functioning of the Body of Christ (Rom. 12:4-5; 1 Cor. 12:7, 12).

Romans 12 and 1 Corinthians 12 list categories of giftedness. Because those lists are somewhat different, I believe they are not intended to be precise, exhaustive lists but general areas in which the Spirit tends to gift people. For example, within the category of teaching you might have many teachers whose teaching styles all differ from one other. The same could be true of preachers, leaders, or any other category of giftedness. (Incidentally, I don't include the miraculous sign gifts—tongues, interpretation of tongues, healing, and miracles—in the general categories of spiritual gifts operative today. I believe those gifts passed away with the apostolic era.)

I like to compare the general categories of spiritual gifts to the primary colors on an artist's pallet, which he blends into various shades. Similarly, God blends the spiritual gifts into the perfect shade for every individual believer. He painted you just the color He wanted you to be. You are a unique combination of the various categories of giftedness.

Peter said, "As each one has received a special gift, employ it in serving one another, as good stewards of the manifold grace of God" (1 Pet. 4:10). Notice the singular use of "gift" there and in 2 Timothy 1:6. Every believer receives the gift that the Spirit designed for him or her, but that gift is a combination of categories blended together to make you unique spiritually. Perhaps that is what is indicated by the plural use of "gifts" elsewhere in Scripture (e.g., Rom. 12:6; 1 Cor. 12:4).

The only way your gift can be known is in the context of the ministry to which God calls you. At the moment of your salvation you received the Holy Spirit (Rom. 8:9), were placed into the Body of Christ (1 Cor. 12:13), and were gifted by the Spirit to minister within the church (1 Cor. 12:11). But those divine enablements are not evident until you begin to minister. In Timothy's case, the combination of preaching, teaching, leading, and doing the work of an evangelist was his gift. It was present within him from the time of his salvation, but it didn't come to fruition until he followed his calling.

When we put our spiritual gifts to good use, God's power works through us more mightily than at any other time.

D. The Reception (v. 6d)

"Through the laying on of my hands."

There has been much discussion about when Timothy received his spiritual gift. Verse 6 implies that it was bestowed on him directly through the laying on of Paul's hands. That interpretation is certainly possible, although spiritual gifts are normally given at the time of salvation. Timothy's case may have been extraordinary because of his unique role in the early church. Perhaps he received his gift at the time of his conversion, but it remained latent until Paul and the presbytery laid hands on him (1 Tim. 4:14) and word concerning him came through prophetic utterance (1 Tim. 1:18). We cannot be sure which view is correct.

By mentioning the laying on of hands, Paul was affirming his personal knowledge of Timothy's giftedness, thereby making Timothy accountable for the use of his gift. His mentioning the presbytery who laid hands on Timothy in 1 Timothy 4:14 had the same effect: it made Timothy accountable to a larger group of men for fulfilling his commission. The same is true of 1 Timothy 1:18 where Paul reminds him that his gift came directly from God. So he was also accountable to God for the way he used it.

Timothy was obligated to God, to his church, and to his mentor for making good use of his spiritual gift. We are similarly obligated. Yet many believers don't understand their spiritual obligations. They act as if Christianity is a spectator sport and their only responsibility is to show up on Sunday, sing a few songs, listen to the sermon, then go home. Those people are missing the very purpose for their existence.

Being unashamed of Christ begins with recognizing that you exist to identify with Christ, exalt Him, and use your gift to serve Him—whatever your gift might be. That gives your life focus and helps bring boldness and courage to your ministry.

How Can You Identify Your Spiritual Gift?

Some Christians find it difficult to identify or define their spiritual gift. Keep in mind it is not important that you be able to precisely define your gift. What matters is that you are ministering in the energy of the Holy Spirit. Your gift is manifested in your ministry, and it is exciting to see what He does with you when you give yourself wholeheartedly to His service.

Even those who understand their spiritual gifts are sometimes concerned about whether they are in the right ministry. But I believe the Spirit gives us the desire to minister in the area of our giftedness. Early in my ministry I attempted to counsel a gentleman. At the conclusion of our second session he said to me, "I want to tell you something that may help you in your future ministry: you don't have the gift of counseling." I responded, "Thank you for that helpful observation. I think you're right. To be truthful, I don't have the desire to counsel people." I was attempting to do something I wasn't gifted to do. On the other hand, my gift is preaching, and that's what I want to do most.

Rather than wondering what your spiritual gift is, examine your desires to see where the Spirit is prompting you to minister. Then ask God to fulfill your desires. If you are walking by the Spirit, your desires will coincide with His will for your part in serving the Body of Christ.

Conclusion

The first safeguard against being ashamed of Christ is renewing your gift. We might call that the discipline of ministry—doing what the Holy Spirit has called and gifted you to do. Don't let the fire get low; keep your heart and mind focused on that sacred task, and your obedience will be a source of boldness and courage.

In our next chapter we will explore the second way to avoid being ashamed of Christ: considering your resources (v. 7). We will see that God is not the source of timidity but of power, love, and discipline. From Him we receive all we need to fulfill our calling. We simply need to use those resources.

Focusing on the Facts

1. What does not being ashamed of Christ mean (see p. 31)?
2. What are some reasons that Christians are sometimes ashamed of Christ (see p. 32)?
3. List three consequences of being ashamed of Christ (see pp. 32-36).
4. How did Jesus restore Peter to ministry (John 21:15-17; see p. 33)?
5. Was Peter's love for Jesus genuine? Explain (John 21:18-19; see pp. 33-34).
6. How did Peter's behavior change after his restoration to ministry (see p. 34)?
7. What did Jesus mean when He said He would confess those who confess Him and deny those who deny Him (Matt. 10:32-33; see pp. 34-35)?

8. A believer who is ashamed of Christ is acting like an _____ (see p. 36).
9. What is the first step in cultivating boldness (see p. 37)?
10. If we neglect our spiritual responsibilities, we have lost sight of our _____ (see p. 37).
11. Why did Paul remind Timothy to rekindle his spiritual gift (1 Tim. 1:5; see p. 37)?
12. Are the lists of spiritual gifts in Romans 12 and 1 Corinthians 12 exhaustive? Explain (see p. 38).
13. When do the divine enablements we receive from God to help us serve Him become evident (see p. 39)?

Pondering the Principles

1. Regretfully, we all have times when we are ashamed to speak of Christ or be identified with Him. Therefore, we must be ever watchful and prayerful not to neglect our source of boldness. Read the following verses, noting the source and results of boldness: Psalm 138:3; Acts 4:31; Ephesians 3:11-12; 6:19-20; and Philippians 1:19-20. Extract the principles in those verses for developing greater boldness and be sure to implement them in your life.

2. Jesus is omniscient, which means He knows everything. Peter said, "Lord, You know all things; You know that I love You" (John 21:17). Even though Peter had denied Him three times, Jesus saw beyond his failures and knew his love was genuine. When our behavior betrays a shallow love for our Lord, it is wonderful to know that He sees our hearts and is ready to forgive and restore us to usefulness as He did with Peter. Be sure to thank Him for His omniscience and grace. And always be ready to forgive others just as Jesus has forgiven you (Eph. 4:32).

3
Not Being Ashamed of Christ—Part 2

Outline

Introduction

Review
I. Renew Your Gift (v. 6)

Lesson
II. Consider Your Resources (v. 7)
    A. Supernatural Power
        1. Its definition
        2. Its source
        3. Its potential
    B. Supernatural Love
        1. Its source
        2. Its characteristics
    C. Supernatural Discipline
        1. Exercising self-control
        2. Applying wisdom
        3. Maintaining priorities
III. Accept Your Sufferings (v. 8a-c)
    A. By Identifying with the Lord Himself (v. 8a)
    B. By Identifying with the Lord's People (v. 8b)
        1. Paul's prominence
        2. Paul's plea
        3. Paul's perspective
    C. By Identifying with the Lord's Standard (v. 8c)

IV. Remember Your God (vv. 8d-10)
  A. He Is Powerful (v. 8d)
    1. God's power is available to us
    2. God's power preserves us
    3. God's power is sovereign
    4. God's power strengthens us
  B. He Saved Us (v. 9a)
    1. God is the author of salvation
    2. God is the preserver of salvation
  C. He Called Us (v. 9b-10b)
    1. To what did He call us?
    2. On what basis did He call us?
    3. When did He call us?
  D. He Abolished Death (v. 10b)
    1. The term defined
    2. The means described
  E. He Gave Us Eternal Life (v. 10c)
    1. The terms defined
    2. The means described

Conclusion

Introduction

In 2 Timothy 1:6-18 the apostle Paul stresses the importance of cultivating courage and boldness in ministry. That's what it means to be unashamed (vv. 8, 12, 16). Courage leads us to proclaim the gospel in an uncompromising way. It motivates us to confront sin and false teaching by "speaking the truth in love" (Eph. 4:15) regardless of the repercussions.

Timothy was ministering in a hostile environment. His identifying with Christ and with Paul could have cost him his freedom or even his life. Therefore Paul exhorted him to "be strong in the grace that is in Christ Jesus" (2 Tim. 2:1). But Paul knew that maintaining steadfastness in a hostile environment required more than a simple instruction to be strong. Timothy needed to understand the rationale for being bold, which Paul explains in 2 Timothy 1:6-18.

Review

I. RENEW YOUR GIFT (v. 6; see pp. 37-41)

"For this reason I remind you to kindle afresh the gift of God which is in you through the laying on of my hands."

Courage rises out of a sense of giftedness. If we know what God has equipped us to do, and understand that His Spirit is ministering through us as we exercise our gifts, we have greater boldness to minister. We also gain a greater sense of purpose because using our gifts is how we make our most significant contribution to the Body of Christ.

Lesson

II. CONSIDER YOUR RESOURCES (v. 7)

"God has not given us a spirit of timidity, but of power and love and discipline."

Some believers lack courage and boldness to minister for Christ because they don't understand their divine resources. They fear they may somehow be cut off from God's power. They are unsure of how long their spiritual extension cord is. But God did not gift us for the advancement of His kingdom and then give us a spirit of timidity (Gk., *deilia*, "cowardice," "fearfulness," "embarrassment," "shame," "weakness," or "frailty") that would negate that gift. Instead He gave us power, love, and discipline to complement and motivate the use of our gift. Weakness on our part indicates that we are not making full use of our spiritual resources.

At the moment of your salvation God deposited power, love, and discipline into your spiritual bank account. As a new believer you received the Holy Spirit, who is the source of supernatural power. Jesus said, "You shall receive power when the Holy Spirit has come upon you" (Acts 1:8). He is also the source of supernatural love. Paul said, "The love of God has been poured out within our hearts through the Holy Spirit who was given to us" (Rom. 5:5). Additionally you received discipline because "the fruit of the Spirit is . . . self-control [discipline]" (Gal. 5:22-23).

Every believer possesses power, love, and discipline. So if we are timid, ineffective, or weak in our ministries, or if we lack courage and boldness to speak for Christ, it is not because we lack divine resources. It is probably due to our own sin, because God has given us the resources to act otherwise.

Let's take a closer look at those resources.

A. Supernatural Power

1. Its definition

The Greek word translated "power" (*dunamis*) means "might" or "dynamic power" and comes from the same root word as the English words *dynamite* and *dynamic*. In the context of 1 Timothy 1, "power" refers to a dynamic spiritual energy that produces results.

2. Its source

God is the source of our supernatural power. It doesn't matter what the opposition is or how powerful the adversary is; the power of God within us will produce results.

But before we can fully benefit from that resource, we must understand its availability. That's why Paul said, "I pray that the eyes of your heart may be enlightened, so that you may know what is the hope of His calling, what are the riches of the glory of His inheritance in the saints, and what is the surpassing greatness of His power toward us who believe. These are in accordance with the working of the strength of His might which He brought about in Christ, when He raised Him from the dead, and seated Him at His right hand in the heavenly places, far above all rule and authority and power and dominion, and every name that is named" (Eph. 1:18-21).

Paul prayed that we would understand that the power at work within us is the same power that overcame death and every other power through Christ's resurrection and ascension.

3. Its potential

Zechariah 4:6 declares, " 'Not by might nor by power, but by My Spirit,' says the Lord of hosts." God was saying that only the Holy Spirit could produce the power to complete the Old Testament Temple. In the same way, only He can produce the necessary power to accomplish God's purposes in the believer's life.

When we operate outside the spiritual dimension, we are limited to our natural abilities. But when we operate in the spiritual dimension, we operate on supernatural power that produces results that otherwise could never be accomplished.

Paul said God is "able to do exceeding abundantly beyond all that we ask or think, according to the power that works within us" (Eph. 3:20). It is marvelous to serve Christ and see His power at work through you as you exalt the Lord and advance His kingdom. Every believer has access to that power by yielding to the Spirit's control.

B. Supernatural Love

1. Its source

The source of supernatural love is the Holy Spirit (Rom. 5:5). When we receive Him, we receive God's love.

2. Its characteristics

Scripture lists several characteristics of God's love.

a) It surpasses knowledge

Paul prayed that the Ephesian Christians, "rooted and grounded in love, [would] be able to comprehend with all the saints what is the breadth and length and height and depth, and . . . know the love of Christ which surpasses knowledge" (Eph. 3:17-19).

b) It restrains power

Power not governed by love can be abrasive, abusive, or injurious. Love establishes the parameters of sensitivity and compassion wherein power can operate to God's glory.

c) It doesn't discriminate

Love permeates every aspect of our ministry, whether it is directed toward God or men. Whoever receives our ministry receives our love.

d) It requires volition

The Greek word translated "love" (*agapē*) describes a volitional rather than an emotional or sensual love. It is the highest kind of love—the love of choice.

e) It makes sacrifices

Agapē manifests itself through self-denial and sacrificial service on behalf of others. It's the quality of love Jesus described in John 15:13: "Greater love has no one than this, that one lay down his life for his friends."

f) It forgives others

Peter said, "Keep fervent in your love for one another, because love covers [forgives or overlooks] a multitude of sins" (1 Pet. 4:8).

g) It overcomes fear

First John 4:18 says, "There is no fear in love; but perfect love casts out fear." If I love something or someone supremely, I lose all desire for self-preservation. For example, if one of my children were to fall into the ocean and begin to drown, my love for that child would cause me to dive in to rescue him with no thought for my own safety. In the same way, if I love God supremely, I will put my life on the line in serving Him and forget all thoughts of self-preservation.

Whatever you love controls your actions. If you love the Lord you will count it gain, rather than loss, if you lose your life in taking the gospel to others or otherwise serving Christ.

However, if you predominantly love yourself, you will do everything possible to preserve your own life-style, comfort, success, and reputation—regardless of God or anyone else. But if you love the Lord God with all your heart, soul, and mind, and your neighbor as yourself (Matt. 22:37, 39), you will fearlessly serve God and others.

How can we love like that? The supernatural resource is present within us. If we walk by the Spirit, we manifest His love in our lives as He produces His fruit within us (Gal. 5:22).

C. Supernatural Discipline

The Greek word translated "discipline" in 2 Timothy 1:7 (*sōphronismos*) appears only here in the New Testament, so we don't have much information from which to determine its exact meaning. But some of its characteristics can be seen by combining its usage in this context with what we know about other related words.

1. Exercising self-control

Sōphronismos has been defined as "control of oneself in face of panic or of passion" (cf. William Barclay, *The Letters to Timothy, Titus, and Philemon* [Philadelphia: Westminster, 1975], pp. 144-45). It is defined as "a sound mind" in the King James Version. That corresponds with related words that speak of one who is free from the influence of demonic forces (Mark 5:15), for example. Such a person is self-controlled and can think, evaluate, and respond appropriately in any circumstance.

2. Applying wisdom

James said, "If any of you lacks wisdom, let him ask of God, who gives to all men generously and without reproach, and it will be given to him" (James 1:5). Proverbs 2:7 says, "He stores up sound wisdom for the upright." *Sōphronismos* as used in 2 Timothy 1:7 speaks of the application of godly wisdom to every circumstance of life for the advancement of God's kingdom.

3. Maintaining priorities

Sōphronismos also implies the ability to prioritize, making the most of every situation. In the words of Paul, you "box in such a way, as not beating the air" (1 Cor. 9:26). You don't waste your life shadowboxing. You take everything that comes into your life and use it for the kingdom's sake. It's a quality required of elders (1 Tim. 3:2), older men (Titus 2:2), and women who serve as deaconesses in the church (1 Tim. 3:11).

I think most Christians desire to maintain their priorities more consistently than they do. The key is to learn to appropriate your supernatural resources because the Holy Spirit is the divine organizer in your life.

Often I've seen people walking around with an organizer in hand to help them manage their schedules, finances, and other items. Although such tools can be helpful, accomplishing work for God's kingdom depends not on the quality of our organizational helps, but on the degree to which we are yielded to the Spirit. Only He can establish and maintain the proper priorities in our hearts.

The truly disciplined, ordered life belongs to those who walk by the Spirit (Gal. 5:16), are filled with the Spirit (Eph. 5:18), and in whom the Word of Christ dwells richly (Col. 3:16).

Available to every believer is the power we need to do God's will, the love we need to minister with sensitivity and compassion, and the discipline we need to bring every aspect of life to bear on advancing the kingdom. Those are not natural endowments. Paul wasn't talking about the kind of power that characterizes the dynamic, aggressive personality. And he wasn't referring to the purely human level of compassionate, thoughtful, sensitive love that some people demonstrate. And the discipline he spoke of was not that of a Marine drill sergeant. Supernatural resources are not produced by heritage, environment, or education. They are given by God Himself to those who love Him.

Paul knew that if Timothy was to maintain courage and boldness in his ministry, he would have to renew his spiritual gift and get a firm grip on his supernatural resources.

III. ACCEPT YOUR SUFFERINGS (v. 8a-c)

"Therefore do not be ashamed of the testimony of our Lord, or of me His prisoner; but join with me in suffering for the gospel."

Everyone who is faithful to identify with the gospel of Jesus Christ will experience some form of persecution and rejection (2 Tim. 3:12). We must expect that and not let it catch us off guard. Christians who attempt to avoid all conflict and hostility are often devastated when it comes their way. Paul's exhortations to Timothy give us three general principles that teach us how to accept our sufferings.

A. By Identifying with the Lord Himself (v. 8a)

"Do not be ashamed of the testimony of our Lord."

One way Timothy could accept his sufferings was boldly to preach Christ at every opportunity, no matter what persecution might come his way. In that way he would be joining with all those who had suffered before him, including the Lord Himself.

The Greek word translated "testimony" (*marturion*) means "witness." "The testimony of our Lord" speaks of the gospel. To identify with the Lord is to take a public stand for the gospel, boldly proclaiming His death and resurrection, warning fallen men and women that they are sinners headed for eternal punishment, and offering them the glorious hope of heaven through faith in Christ.

Verse 8 does not necessarily imply that Timothy had failed to proclaim the gospel. However, Paul had firsthand knowledge of the serious and potentially deadly stigma of being identified with Christ. He knew things could become very difficult for Timothy in the midst of a society that viewed Jesus as a crucified criminal and Christians as little more than rebellious insurrectionists. It could have been —and still can be—both humiliating and fatal to be identified with Christ. Remaining steadfast in his ministry would demand that Timothy accept his sufferings.

B. By Identifying with the Lord's People (v. 8*b*)

"Or of me His prisoner; but join with me."

1. Paul's prominence

    Second only to the danger of being associated with Christ was the danger of being associated with Paul. Since Paul was the leading spokesman for Christ, all who identified with him exposed themselves to the same dangers he faced.

2. Paul's plea

    Paul admonished Timothy not to be ashamed to identify with him or (by implication) with others who had suffered for preaching Christ. The English phrase "join with me in suffering" is derived from one Greek compound verb that speaks of suffering with others or accepting one's share of evil treatment.

    Second Timothy 3:12 says, "All who desire to live godly in Christ Jesus will be persecuted." We must expect persecution because that is how a hostile world reacts to those who confront it with the true gospel. However, if you never confront sin or if you present the gospel as only a means by which people can have their problems solved, live a happy life, and go to heaven, you may never experience persecution. But if you are bold, you can expect to suffer. In so doing you join with every other persecuted believer throughout history in a blessed fellowship of suffering saints.

3. Paul's perspective

    Paul saw himself as the Lord's prisoner, not as a prisoner of Rome. He knew that Christ sovereignly controlled his life, so if Christ wanted him in prison, he accepted that and believed that he could accomplish a ministry there.

Acts 5:41 says that after the apostles were flogged by some of the Jewish religious leaders, they rejoiced that they had been considered worthy to suffer shame for Christ's name. Paul wanted Timothy to have that attitude and to identify with others who were being persecuted for their faith. We are to have that attitude as well.

C. By Identifying with the Lord's Standard (v. 8c)

"Suffering for the gospel."

Our suffering should always result from our righteousness, not our sinfulness. Peter said, "If you are reviled for the name of Christ, you are blessed, because the Spirit of glory and of God rests upon you. By no means let any of you suffer as a murderer, or thief, or evildoer, or a troublesome meddler; but if anyone suffers as a Christian, let him not feel ashamed, but in that name let him glorify God" (1 Pet. 4:14-16).

When you suffer for the gospel, don't be fearful or feel as if Christ has deserted you. Instead, understand that you have been counted worthy to suffer for Him. It is an honor! Paul said, "I bear on my body the brand marks of Jesus" (Gal. 6:17). He considered it a privilege to be beaten with whips and rods and to bear scars from the manacles on his hands and feet for his Lord's sake (2 Cor. 11:23-28). It was a given element in his ministry. In Ephesians 3:1 he calls himself "the prisoner of Christ Jesus." Wherever Christ took him is where he wanted to be.

As we serve the Lord, we can expect persecution. And an important element in developing greater courage and boldness is learning to accept our sufferings by identifying with the Lord, with His people, and with His standard. Then when persecution comes, we will have the confidence to know that God is counting us worthy to share in the sufferings of Christ.

IV. REMEMBER YOUR GOD (vv. 8d-10)

"According to the power of God, who has saved us, and called us with a holy calling, not according to our works, but according to His own purpose and grace which was granted us in Christ Jesus from all eternity, but now has been revealed by the appearing of our Savior Christ Jesus, who abolished death, and brought life and immortality to light through the gospel."

That is one of the greatest statements on the doctrine of salvation in Scripture! It reminds us that as we minister, we must not forget the God who upholds us.

A. He Is Powerful (v. 8d)

"According to the power of God."

To suffer according to the power of God implies an understanding of four key aspects of God's power.

1. God's power is available to us

   God is almighty and makes available to each believer the power to endure every trial.

2. God's power preserves us

   If He so wills, God can overwhelm our enemies and preserve us in the midst of persecution. Millions of Christians have faced suffering with that confidence. Even when some have lost their lives, God's kingdom has been advanced.

3. God's power is sovereign

   God sovereignly permits us to suffer so that our faith can mature (James 1:2-4). He can stop persecution at any time He chooses. If He allows it to continue, He does so for our good and His glory.

4. God's power strengthens us

   Jesus said, "All [power] has been given to Me in heaven and on earth" (Matt. 28:18). He then promised that the

Holy Spirit would empower His disciples for ministry (Acts 1:8). That's true of every believer. Paul said, "I can do all things through [Christ] who strengthens me" (Phil. 4:13). Jude said that God "is able to keep you from stumbling, and to make you stand in the presence of His glory blameless with great joy" (Jude 24).

B. He Saved Us (v. 9a)

"Who has saved us."

1. God is the author of salvation

   Salvation is because of God. He designed, initiated, and effected it on our behalf. In so doing He delivered us from sin, death, Satan, and hell. That is a powerful work! Before the foundation of the world, He chose those whom He would redeem (Eph. 1:4), and in Christ He brought His plan to fruition.

2. God is the preserver of salvation

   Because God has the power to save us, we have confidence that He can keep us. Romans 5:10 says, "If while we were enemies, we were reconciled to God through the death of His Son, much more, having been reconciled, we shall be saved by His life." That's why all who are saved will ultimately be glorified (Rom. 8:30).

   Jesus said, "This is the will of Him who sent Me, that of all that He has given Me I lose nothing, but raise it up on the last day. For this is the will of My Father, that everyone who beholds the Son, and believes in Him, may have eternal life; and I Myself will raise him up on the last day" (John 6:39-40). He also said, "My sheep hear My voice, and I know them, and they follow Me; and I give eternal life to them, and they shall never perish; and no one shall snatch them out of My hand" (John 10:27-28). Jesus saved us, and He will preserve us.

C. He Called Us (v. 9*b*-10*a*)

"[God] called us with a holy calling, not according to our works, but according to His own purpose and grace which was granted us in Christ Jesus from all eternity, but now has been revealed by the appearing of our Savior Christ Jesus."

1. To what did He call us?

God not only saved us from sin but also called us to a holy calling. The Greek word translated "called" here refers to God's effectual, saving call, not to His invitation. It isn't His general call to all sinners to repent.

God saved us from sin so that we might be holy. He transformed us from sinners to saints, making us new creatures in Christ (2 Cor. 5:17). Otherwise we could never experience His holiness.

2. On what basis did He call us?

You can do nothing to earn salvation. Paul said, "By the works of the Law no flesh will be justified in His sight" (Rom. 3:20). Ephesians 2:8-9 says, "By grace you have been saved through faith; and that not of yourselves, it is the gift of God; not as a result of works, that no one should boast." Titus 3:5 says, "He saved us, not on the basis of deeds which we have done in righteousness, but according to His mercy." Our salvation is entirely the work of God.

Since God saved us and made us holy without our help, He will also preserve us without our help. We can serve Him with abandon and trust Him to care for us. We can speak God's truth in love (Eph. 4:15). Our responsibility is to be faithful to our calling.

Scripture teaches that "[God] chose us in [Christ] before the foundation of the world" (Eph. 1:4) and that He wrote our names in the Lamb's Book of Life (Rev. 21:27). That means God purposed to redeem us before the world began, as our text in 2 Timothy affirms: He "saved us . . . according to His own purpose and grace which was granted us in Christ Jesus from all eternity" (v. 9). Paul mentioned grace because there's no other way for us to be saved. In this context grace refers to undeserved forgiveness, which is an essential element in salvation.

3. When did He call us?

As verse 9 says, God's eternal purpose and grace were granted to us "from all eternity." That literally means "from before eternal times," which is beyond our finite comprehension. Our destiny was sealed before the universe was created.

That we were granted salvation in Christ Jesus before time began presupposes Christ's eternal preexistence and deity. He had to be there along with the Father.

God conceived of our redemption before time but revealed it in history by "the appearing of our Savior Christ Jesus" (v. 10). The Greek word translated "appearing" (*epiphaneia*) is used elsewhere in the pastoral epistles to refer to Christ's second coming (1 Tim. 6:14; 2 Tim. 4:1, 8; Titus 2:13), but here it clearly refers to His resurrection because verse 10 says Christ abolished death. Our salvation was revealed in the resurrection of Christ.

Notice that Paul referred to Christ as "our Savior" (v. 10). In the pastoral epistles he most often used that title with reference to God the Father, but here it refers to the Son. Since there is no Savior besides God (Isa. 43:11; Hos. 13:4), Paul is clearly equating Jesus with God.

D. He Abolished Death (v. 10*b*)

"Who abolished death."

1. The term defined

The Greek word translated "abolish" (*katargeō*) means "to render inoperative." It doesn't mean that death is nonexistent but that the power and sting of death have been removed for believers. We don't have to fear death

because Christ has transformed it from a dreaded enemy to a welcomed friend.

Paul explained, "To live is Christ, and to die is gain.
. . . [I have] the desire to depart and be with Christ, for
that is very much better" (Phil. 1:21-23). Like Paul, we
long for the day when "this perishable [body] will have
put on the imperishable, and this mortal [body] will
have put on immortality, then will come about the saying that is written, 'Death is swallowed up in victory. O
death, where is your victory? O death, where is your
sting?' The sting of death is sin, and the power of sin is
the law; but thanks be to God, who gives us the victory
through our Lord Jesus Christ" (1 Cor. 15:54-57). We are
"longing to be clothed with our dwelling from heaven"
(2 Cor. 5:2).

2. The means described

The heart of the gospel is the death and resurrection of
Christ. And in His resurrection He appeared as the One
who had abolished death. Hebrews 2:14-15 says that
Christ partook of flesh and blood "that through death
He might render powerless him who had the power of
death, that is, the devil; and might deliver those who
through fear of death were subject to slavery all their
lives."

E. He Gave Us Eternal Life (v. 10c)

"And brought life and immortality to light through the
gospel."

1. The terms defined

"Life and immortality" refer to the eternal, immortal life
that believers will have in the presence of God because
they have been saved.

2. The means described

Faith in the gospel, which is the good news that Jesus
died and rose again, is the means by which we gain
eternal life.

Conclusion

Throughout the New Testament the resurrection of Christ stands as the hallmark of God's power. As we renew our spiritual gift, appropriate our resources, and accept our sufferings, we need to remember our God, confident that His power is more than sufficient to bring about ultimate victory. After all, He saved us from sin, death, and hell; transformed us into holy creatures in Christ; planned our salvation from before eternity; brought that plan to fruition by the death and resurrection of Christ; abolished the power of death; and gave us eternal life. Such power can surely preserve us as we minister in His Name. So take courage and serve Christ with boldness!

Focusing on the Facts

1. Some believers lack courage and boldness to minister for Christ because they don't understand their _____ _____ (see p. 45).
2. According to 2 Timothy 1:7, what specific resources has God given to every believer (see p. 45)?
3. Define "power" as used in 2 Timothy 1:7 (see p. 46).
4. What promise do we find in Ephesians 3:20 (see p. 47)?
5. List and explain seven characteristics of supernatural love (see pp. 47-48).
6. What does "discipline" in 2 Timothy 1:7 appear to mean (see pp. 49-50)?
7. Everyone who is faithful to identify with the gospel of Jesus Christ will experience some form of _____ and _____ (see p. 51).
8. Identify three principles that help us accept our sufferings (2 Tim. 1:8; see pp. 51-53).
9. What does "the testimony of our Lord" (2 Tim. 1:8) speak of (see p. 51)?
10. What does it mean to identify with the Lord (see p. 51)?
11. Does Paul's admonition not to be ashamed of the Lord (2 Tim. 1:8) imply that Timothy had stopped proclaiming the gospel? Explain (see pp. 51-52).
12. What was Paul's perspective on his imprisonment (2 Tim. 1:8; see pp. 52-53)?
13. How did the apostles react to persecution (Acts 5:41; see p. 53)?

14. Our suffering should always result from our _____, not our _____ (see p. 53).
15. What does it mean to suffer "according to the power of God" (2 Tim. 1:8; see pp. 54-55)?
16. Because God has the power to _____ us, we have confidence that He can _____ us (see p. 55).
17. What does Jesus promise in John 6:39-40 (see p. 55)?
18. Define "called" as used in 2 Timothy 1:9 (see p. 56).
19. On what basis did God call us (2 Tim. 1:9; see pp. 56-57)?
20. When were believers first included in God's redemptive plan (2 Tim. 1:9; see p. 57)?
21. What is the significance of the term "Savior" as applied to Jesus in 2 Timothy 1:10 (see p. 57)?
22. In what sense has death been abolished (2 Tim. 1:10; see pp. 57-58)?
23. By what means did Christ abolish death (see p. 58)?
24. Define "life and immortality" as used in 2 Timothy 1:10 (see p. 58).

Pondering the Principles

1. Maintaining proper priorities is one aspect of the discipline God gives us through the Holy Spirit (2 Tim. 1:7; see p. 50). Have you given careful thought to your priorities lately? Are they consistent with Scripture? For example, do you love God supremely (Matt. 22:37)? Do you realize the surpassing value of knowing Christ and of maturing in your relationship with Him (Phil. 3:8)? Do you value God's kingdom and righteousness more than the temporal things of life (Matt. 6:33)? Do you love others as much or more than you love yourself (Matt. 22:39)? Do you make disciples in Christ's name and teach them God's Word (Matt. 28:19-20)? Remember, you reveal your true priorities in the way you spend your time and resources.

2. Suffering is an effective tool that God uses to strengthen our character and teach us greater dependence on Him. But sometimes in the midst of suffering we lose our perspective and forget God's ability to use every circumstance for our good and His glory. Reviewing the biblical principles for dealing with suffering is a good way to avoid falling prey to discouragement and frustration. Read the following verses, noting God's perspective

on your suffering. And thank Him that no matter what the circumstances, He is still in control.

- The inevitability of suffering (2 Tim. 3:12)
- The extent of our suffering (1 Cor. 10:13)
- The pattern for enduring suffering (1 Thess. 1:6; 2:14-15; 1 Pet. 2:21-23; 4:12-16, 19)
- The results of our suffering (Matt. 5:11-12; Phil. 1:6; James 1:2-4)

4
Not Being Ashamed of Christ—Part 3

Outline

Introduction
A. An Example of Courage
B. A Need for Zeal

Review
  I. Renew Your Gift (v. 6)
 II. Consider Your Resources (v. 7)
III. Accept Your Sufferings (v. 8a-c)
 IV. Remember Your God (vv. 8d-10)

Lesson
  V. Realize Your Duty (vv. 11-12a)
      A. The Beginning of Paul's Duty (v. 11a)
          1. His appointment
          2. His attitude
              a) Self-sacrifice
              b) Compulsion
      B. The Nature of Paul's Duty (v. 11b)
          1. He was a preacher
          2. He was an apostle
          3. He was a teacher
      C. The Consequence of Paul's Duty (v. 12a)
 VI. Be Steadfast (v. 12b-d)
      A. The Object of Our Trust (12b)
      B. The Result of Our Trust (v. 12c)
      C. The Culmination of Our Trust (v. 12d)
VII. Affirm Your Doctrine (vv. 13-14)
      A. Grasp the Truth (v. 13)
      B. Guard the Truth (v. 14)

Introduction

A. An Example of Courage

I remember reading that, during the terrible Boxer Rebellion in China at the turn of this century, insurgents captured a mission station, blocked all the gates but one, and placed a cross flat on the ground in front of it. Word was passed to those inside that any who trampled the cross under foot would be free to go but that any refusing would be shot to death.

Terribly frightened, the first seven people trampled the cross under their feet and were allowed to go free. But the eighth, a young girl, refused to commit such an act. Kneeling beside the cross in prayer for strength, she arose, moved carefully around the cross, and went out to face the firing squad. Strengthened by her example, every one of the substantial number remaining followed her to their deaths.

That's a tremendous example of the powerful influence of a courageous life. The apostle Paul set that kind of example for Timothy—and for us—and exhorted him to be bold for Christ no matter what.

B. A Need for Zeal

Such boldness requires a zealous commitment to Christ and to biblical truth. That may seem fanatical, but it's no less a commitment than the world demonstrates for its sinful pursuits. Sadly, there seem to be relatively few Christians whose lives are bold and uncompromising testimonies to the power and grace of God. Shouldn't we be more zealous for righteousness than the world is for sin?

That's the kind of commitment Paul calls for in 2 Timothy 1:6-18. Timothy may have needed that exhortation because he was weakening under the pressure of correcting the many errors in the Ephesian church. Additionally, there was the threat of Roman persecution. Many Christians would be imprisoned and put to death, including Paul.

Timothy was especially vulnerable because of his close association with Paul. So Paul wanted to strengthen him and encourage him to carry on the ministry.

Review

Paul's exhortation to Timothy suggests eight ways to live a life of boldness and confidence.

I. RENEW YOUR GIFT (v. 6; see pp. 37-41)

II. CONSIDER YOUR RESOURCES (v. 7; see pp. 45-51)

III. ACCEPT YOUR SUFFERINGS (v. 8a-c; see pp. 51-53)

The contemporary heresy of the health, wealth, and prosperity gospel has deceived many people into thinking that the purpose of Christianity is to provide believers with happy, healthy, prosperous, and trouble-free lives. If that is your view of Christianity, your theology will be severely shaken when suffering and persecution come your way. You will be tempted to doubt God because suffering is contrary to what you expect from Him.

Scripture says all who desire to live godly lives will suffer persecution (2 Tim. 3:12). That's because people who do not want to deal with their sin cannot tolerate God's Word or His people. Loyalty to Christ causes conflict with His enemies, so make any needed adjustments in your theology and learn to expect opposition and persecution.

IV. REMEMBER YOUR GOD (vv. 8d-10; see pp. 54-59)

God didn't need our help when He saved us and made us holy, and He doesn't need our help to preserve us. Rather than concerning ourselves with self-preservation, we can confidently entrust our lives to Him, knowing that He will care for us.

Peter said, "Let those . . . who suffer according to the will of God entrust their souls to a faithful Creator in doing what is right" (1 Pet. 4:19). That's what Shadrach, Meshach, and Abednego did when they faced King Nebuchadnezzar's fiery furnace. They said, "If it be so, our God whom we serve is able to deliver us from the furnace of blazing fire; and He will deliver us out of your hand, O king" (Dan. 3:17). Paul said, "I can do all things through [Christ] who strengthens me" (Phil. 4:13).

That's what it means to remember your God. And if you approach ministry in that way, you will have great boldness and courage.

Lesson

V. REALIZE YOUR DUTY (vv. 11-12a)

A. The Beginning of Paul's Duty (v. 11a)

"For which I was appointed."

1. His appointment

   Paul knew that Christ Himself had appointed him to the ministry. That realization gave Paul a profound sense of duty that motivated everything he did.

The Greek word translated "appointed" (*tithēmi*) here speaks of a divine commission. Paul's commission came while he was traveling to Damascus to persecute Christians (Acts 9:3-6). After confronting Paul directly, the Lord revealed that Paul was chosen to bear His name "before the Gentiles and kings and the sons of Israel" (Acts 9:15).

2. His attitude

a) Self-sacrifice

In Acts 20:24 Paul says, "I do not consider my life of any account as dear to myself, in order that I may finish my course, and the ministry which I received from the Lord Jesus, to testify solemnly of the gospel of the grace of God." He didn't concern himself with self-preservation. He had a solemn duty to perform.

The same was true of the other apostles, whom Jesus commissioned to "go . . . and make disciples of all the nations, baptizing them in the name of the Father and the Son and the Holy Spirit, teaching them to observe all that [He had] commanded" (Matt. 28:19-20). The apostle Paul fulfilled that commission quite literally. From the start it was clear that he would endure much suffering in so doing (Acts 9:16).

b) Compulsion

In Colossians 1:23 Paul says, "I . . . was made a minister." He didn't choose his ministry; he was appointed by the Lord Himself. He told the Corinthians, "If I preach the gospel, I have nothing to boast of, for I am under compulsion; for woe is me if I do not preach the gospel. . . . I buffet my body and make it my slave, lest possibly, after I have preached to others, I myself should be disqualified" (1 Cor. 9:16, 27).

Paul sought no commendation from others, because he was under compulsion to preach. And he was so committed to fulfilling his duty that he carefully disciplined himself to avoid being disqualified from the ministry by some sin.

B. The Nature of Paul's Duty (v. 11*b*)

"A preacher and an apostle and a teacher."

1. He was a preacher

Paul's function was that of a preacher—one who proclaims, heralds, or announces a message publicly.

2. He was an apostle

Paul's authority was that of an apostle—one who was chosen directly by Jesus Christ to be His messenger.

3. He was a teacher

Paul's content was that of a teacher—one who disseminates God's truth.

Paul was sent as an apostle to proclaim the truth of God.

C. The Consequence of Paul's Duty (v. 12*a*)

"For this reason I also suffer."

Paul suffered severely for preaching the gospel. In Galatians 6:17 he says, "I bear on my body the brand marks of Jesus." The enemies of Christ couldn't get to Him any more so they vented their wrath on Paul. In 2 Corinthians 11:23-27 he gives a list of things he endured for the sake of Christ, including stoning and being beaten with whips and rods.

Why Is Ministry Sometimes Sorrowful?

Spiritual duty is a bittersweet thing. It brings a mixture of joy and sorrow. There are several factors that account for the sorrowful aspect of ministry.

1. Persecution

Paul loved his ministry, yet he suffered great persecution as a result of it.

2. Judgment

In Revelation 10:9 the apostle John is instructed to eat a scroll. It was sweet in his mouth because it was God's Word, but bitter in his stomach because it spoke of God's severe judgment upon sinners (vv. 9-11).

3. Unrighteousness

The nineteenth-century English preacher Charles H. Spurgeon said, "A man shall carry a bucket of water on his head and be very tired with the burden; but that same man when he dives into the sea shall have a thousand buckets on his head without perceiving their weight, because he is in the element and it entirely surrounds him. The duties of holiness are very irksome to men who are not in the element of holiness; but when once those men are cast into the element of grace, then they bear ten times more, and feel no weight, but are refreshed thereby with joy unspeakable" (cited by Elon Foster, *New Cyclopedia of Prose Illustrations* [N.Y.: Thomas Y. Crowell, 1872]).

Spiritual duty can be a tremendous burden if you're not living a holy life. But with holiness comes grace to minister in the power of the Spirit and joy to lift your heart.

4. Neglect

A duty fulfilled brings joy; a duty neglected brings pain. I know of men whose lives have been shattered because they failed to fulfill their spiritual duties. Their failure eats at their conscience, destroys their peace of mind, and robs them of any sense of meaningful achievement.

Are you living a holy life and faithfully discharging your spiritual duties? Remember, our "momentary, light affliction is producing for us an eternal weight of glory far beyond all comparison" (2 Cor. 4:17).

VI. BE STEADFAST (v. 12b-d)

A. The Object of Our Trust (12b)

"I am not ashamed; for I know whom I have believed."

The Greek word translated "know" (*oida*) means perceiving something with your senses and concluding that it is true. Paul personally knew the One in whom he placed his trust. Verse 12 could be a reference to God the Father or to the Savior Christ Jesus (v. 10). I believe it is a general reference to both.

Notice he did not say, "I know *what* I have believed," but, "I know *whom* I have believed." Paul was sustained not by his understanding of theology alone but by his relationship with God.

B. The Result of Our Trust (v. 12c)

"I am convinced that He is able to guard what I have entrusted to Him."

Paul was nearing the end of his life. Throughout his years of ministry he had seen the power of God at work over and over again in redeeming the lost and healing the sick. He had seen Jesus and had ascended to the third heaven, seeing things too wonderful to speak of (2 Cor. 12:2-4). He had an intimate relationship with God and knew nothing could ever separate him from the love of Christ (Rom. 8:38-39).

All his experiences and observations led him to conclude that God was able to guard the deposit he had made with Him. What was that deposit? His entire life: soul, ministry, time, and future hope. Everything! He simply gave his life to God and then went about his ministry.

C. The Culmination of Our Trust (v. 12d)

"Until that day."

In 2 Timothy 1:18 Paul says, "The Lord grant to [Onesiphorus] to find mercy from the Lord on that day." In

2 Timothy 4:8 he says, "In the future there is laid up for me the crown of righteousness, which the Lord, the righteous Judge, will award to me on that day; and not only to me, but also to all who have loved His appearing."

It refers to the day when the Lord comes to reward His church and give to each believer a crown of righteousness. That will occur at the Judgment Seat of Christ (Rom. 14:10; 2 Cor. 5:10), sometime after the rapture of the church. In Revelation 22:12 Jesus says, "Behold, I am coming quickly, and My reward is with Me, to render to every man according to what he has done."

Paul trusted God's ability to keep him until that special day when he would receive his eternal reward. We find that same confidence echoed by Jude: "To Him who is able to keep you from stumbling, and to make you stand in the presence of His glory blameless with great joy . . . be glory . . . now and forever" (vv. 24-25). Both men knew that none could snatch them out of God's hand (John 10:28-29) and that Jesus would keep them and raise them up on the last day (John 6:39).

What a great assurance to know that God keeps us saved! We don't have to manipulate our circumstances to make things work out right. Just imagine the fear and concern you would have if God didn't keep you secure in your salvation. But your life is secure with Him; even the demons cannot overcome you (1 John 4:4).

VII. AFFIRM YOUR DOCTRINE (vv. 13-14)

A. Grasp the Truth (v. 13)

"Retain the standard of sound words which you have heard from me, in the faith and love which are in Christ Jesus."

The Greek word translated "retain" means "to hold tightly" or "grasp." "Standard" is a structure, outline, model, or pattern. "Sound words" is a reference to the wholesome, life-giving words of true doctrine (cf. 1 Tim. 4:6; 6:3).

71

Timothy was to hold tightly to the doctrine that had been entrusted to him (1 Tim. 6:20) by accurately interpreting and applying God's Word. That cultivates spiritual growth and strong theological convictions.

Do You Have the Courage of Your Convictions?

The reason many don't have the courage of their convictions is that they don't have convictions. Before you can put your life on the line for anything, you have to believe in it. But we live in a time when many Christians lack strong, definitive theological convictions. In fact, if you hold firmly to strong doctrine, many people assume you're unloving and antagonistic. That is because much of today's preaching is shallow and many people have been lulled into spiritual complacency. They prefer to hear things that make them feel good about themselves rather than sound doctrine.

But people with strong convictions tend to be bold. That's the attitude Paul wanted to instill in Timothy (2 Timothy 1:7, 13). Do you have the courage of your convictions?

The doctrine Timothy was to guard was the inspired apostolic teaching he had received directly from Paul. He was to hold it in "faith and love" (v. 13). Faith speaks of trust in God. That leads to firm and unwavering beliefs. James said, "The one who doubts is like the surf of the sea driven and tossed by the wind . . . unstable in all his ways" (James 1:6-8). Don't be like that. Be assured that what you believe is true. Also, Ephesians 4:15 tells us to speak "the truth in love." We should not have a loveless, cold, insensitive orthodoxy. Instead we are to be sensitive yet uncompromising.

B. Guard the Truth (v. 14)

"Guard, through the Holy Spirit who dwells in us, the treasure which has been entrusted to you."

The Greek word translated "guard" means "to keep safe" or "preserve from corruption or destruction." Romans 8:9 says, "If anyone does not have the Spirit of Christ, he does not belong to Him." Every believer is indwelt by the

Spirit and empowered by Him to guard the treasure that God has entrusted to him or her.

The Greek word translated "treasure" speaks of God's truth as revealed in His Word. Guarding or accurately representing God's Word is the primary task of every believer (1 Tim. 6:20-21).

Is God's Word Secure with You?

As a Christian you are secure with God. But is His Word secure with you? Can He count on you to guard and dispense it as you should?

Sad to say, many churches, seminaries, colleges, and professing Christians have defected from biblical truth. It's fearful to consider the accounting that awaits them for failing to guard what God entrusted to them.

Guarding the Word is the most solemn responsibility we have. But sadly, people who take seriously that sacred trust are becoming increasingly scarce. And those who develop strong biblical convictions must be prepared for the inevitable times of conflict that come to people of conviction. For example, when relatives come to visit, you might have disagreements because you have strong biblical convictions about certain issues on which they vacillate.

Can God rely on you to accurately and lovingly defend His Word even when it involves personal sacrifice on your part?

VIII. CHOOSE YOUR ASSOCIATES CAREFULLY (vv. 15-18)

In 2 Timothy 1:15-18 we see two groups of people: those who were ashamed of Christ and those who weren't. The implication is that we must choose which group we associate with. That is an important issue because our associates influence our behavior. First Corinthians 15:33 says, "Do not be deceived: 'Bad company corrupts good morals.' " Courageous people will help you gain boldness, whereas weak people will rob you of your courage.

What Group Are You Identified With?

The way you live your Christian life identifies you with a group of people who live the same way you do. I want to be identified with the faithful Old Testament saints described in Hebrews 11, the New Testament saints, and the great missionaries and faithful saints of God throughout the centuries. What group do you want to be identified with?

    A. Beware of the Unfaithful (v. 15)

"You are aware of the fact that all who are in Asia turned away from me, among whom are Phygelus and Hermogenes."

Timothy was ministering in Ephesus, a key city in Asia Minor, so he was aware of the defection that Paul mentioned, and probably knew Phygelus and Hermogenes.

    1. Their defection

All who were in Asia Minor had deserted Paul. Apparently they were fearful that identifying with him would lead to their own imprisonment. Their actions were reminiscent of Peter's when he denied Jesus with an oath (Matt. 26:72). They were ashamed and cowardly, thinking only of their own protection.

Paul mentioned two of the defectors by name: Phygelus and Hermogenes. We don't know any more about them. Perhaps they were leaders in one of the churches in Asia Minor, maybe even in Ephesus. They probably ministered alongside Paul but when the persecution started, they quickly disassociated themselves from him.

    2. Paul's reaction

      a) He felt betrayed

One of the painful aspects of ministry is when people whom you have nurtured abandon you amidst difficult circumstances. Such people also become very critical.

That is the pain Paul certainly felt when those in Asia Minor abandoned him. They refused to identify with him even though he had risked his life to bring the gospel to them and had sacrificed his time and strength to teach them God's Word. His only motive was that Christ be formed in them (Gal. 4:19).

Paul was obviously grieved by their defection. No wonder there was such loneliness in his words as he expressed his longing for Timothy's companionship (2 Tim. 1:4).

b) He confronted them openly

Paul didn't let Phygelus and Hermogenes off the hook by hiding or denying their actions. In fact, his mentioning their names identifies them forever in Holy Writ as defectors.

First Timothy 5:20 says, "Those [elders] who continue in sin, rebuke in the presence of all, so that the rest also may be fearful of sinning." Perhaps Phygelus and Hermogenes were elders. By making their defection public knowledge, Paul was enshrining them in the spiritual Hall of Shame (which, among others, includes Demas—2 Tim. 4:10).

B. Adhere to the Faithful (vv. 16-18)

"The Lord grant mercy to the house of Onesiphorus for he often refreshed me, and was not ashamed of my chains; but when he was in Rome, he eagerly searched for me, and found me—the Lord grant to him to find mercy from the Lord on that day and you know very well what services he rendered at Ephesus."

The second group is represented by Onesiphorus and his household—godly people who were characterized by boldness and self-sacrifice. We know they lived in Ephesus because Timothy was ministering there, and in 2 Tim-

75

othy 4:19 Paul instructs him to "greet the household of Onesiphorus."

1. Their ministry to Paul

    Onesiphorus and his family were not ashamed of Paul. Their kindness prompted Paul to pray that the Lord would grant them a special reward.

    They were eager to come alongside Paul to provide some encouraging personal ministry whenever the opportunity arose. Even Paul's "chains" (a reference not only to Paul's handcuffs or manacles but to his state of imprisonment in general) didn't deter Onesiphorus from ministering to him.

    Onesiphorus traveled to Rome and eagerly searched for Paul until he found him. He may have been in Rome on business or perhaps he went there specifically to minister to Paul. In either case he was unashamed and undaunted.

2. Their ministry to the church

    Onesiphorus also ministered to the church at Ephesus. We don't know what his specific role was. He may have been an elder or pastor. Whatever role he had, the quality of his character and service was well-known to Timothy.

Those are the two groups: the unfaithful, who are ashamed of Christ, and the faithful, who are bold. The distinctions are quite clear. To which group to you belong?

Conclusion

Paul wanted Timothy to "be strong in the grace that is in Christ Jesus" (2 Tim. 2:1) by renewing his spiritual gift, understanding his resources, accepting his sufferings, remembering his God, realizing his duty, remaining steadfast, and choosing his associates carefully.

A. The Boldness of Martin Luther

During the Reformation period, Martin Luther exemplified that kind of strength when he stood against the abuses of the Roman Catholic church and the political system it influenced. It has been asserted that he was perhaps as fearless a man as has ever lived. When he set out for the city of Worms to face his accusers, many feared for his life and attempted to dissuade him. "But Luther had set his face to go up to Jerusalem," writes biographer Roland H. Bainton, "and would not be turned aside. He would enter Worms though there were as many devils as tiles on the roofs. . . . He disregarded all human considerations and threw himself utterly upon God" (*Here I Stand: A Life of Martin Luther* [N.Y.: Abingdon, 1950], p. 181).

Once at Worms he wrote, "So long as Christ is merciful, I will not recant a single jot or tittle" (James M. Kittelson, *Luther the Reformer* [Minneapolis: Augsburg, 1986], p. 161). Luther's concluding reply to his accusers was, "Unless I am convicted by Scripture and plain reason—I do not accept the authority of popes and councils, for they have contradicted each other—my conscience is captive to the Word of God. I cannot and I will not recant anything, for to go against conscience is neither right nor safe. God help me. Amen. . . . Here I stand, I cannot do otherwise" (Bainton, p. 185). Afterwards one of the officials remarked, "Dr. Martin spoke wonderfully before the emperor, the princes, and the estates . . . but he is too daring for me" (Bainton, p. 186).

B. The Boldness of King Hezekiah

King Hezekiah of Judah also demonstrated great courage and boldness. When facing a great enemy, he said to his people, "Be strong and courageous, do not fear or be dismayed because of the king of Assyria, nor because of all the multitude which is with him; for the one with us is greater than the one with him. With him is only an arm of flesh, but with us is the Lord our God to help us and to fight our battles" (2 Chron. 32:7-8).

We too can have that kind of confidence when we understand that God Himself has equipped us and is working through us to accomplish His will. So don't be ashamed of Christ. Be bold and courageous!

Focusing on the Facts

1. Define "appointed" as used in 2 Timothy 1:11 (see p. 67).
2. Under what circumstances was Paul commissioned to the ministry (Acts 9:3-6; see p. 67)?
3. Identify two aspects of Paul's attitude toward his duty (see pp. 67-68).
4. What was the threefold nature of Paul's duty (2 Tim. 1:11; see p. 68)?
5. List four factors that can bring sorrow as we minister (see pp. 68-69).
6. Define "know" as used in 2 Timothy 1:12 (see p. 70).
7. What deposit did Paul make with God (2 Tim. 1:12; see p. 71)?
8. What promise does Jesus make in John 6:39 (see p. 71)?
9. What does it mean to "retain the standard of sound words" (2 Tim. 1:13; see pp. 71-72)?
10. Why do many people lack the courage of their convictions (see p. 72)?
11. How does James 1:6-8 describe one who lacks faith (see p. 72)?
12. What is the primary task of every believer (2 Tim. 1:14; see p. 73)?
13. How did Paul react to the defection of Phygelus and Hermogenes (2 Tim. 1:15; see pp. 74-75)?
14. How did Onesiphorus minister to Paul (2 Tim. 1:16-17; see p. 76)?
15. What was Martin Luther's response when called on to recant his belief in justification by faith (see p. 77)?

Pondering the Principles

1. Shadrach, Meshach, and Abednego had the courage to stand up for their convictions, so when their faith was tested they stood firm for the Lord. Read Daniel 3:1-30. What was King Nebuchadnezzar's command (vv. 4-5)? What were the consequences for disobedience (v. 6)? How did Shadrach, Meshach, and Abed-

nego express their faith (vv. 12, 16-18)? How did God honor their faith (v. 27)? What was Nebuchadnezzar's reaction (vv. 28-30)? In what ways has God tested your faith recently? Have your responses demonstrated courage? If not, what specific things can you do to increase your boldness for Christ?

2. Christians are not exempt from our society's relentless quest for instant gratification. Consequently we can be discouraged if we don't quickly see results in our ministries or if things in general don't go our way. But Paul knew that God works on a different timetable. The hope of future rewards gave him courage and strength during times of great stress (2 Tim. 4:8). So rather than dwelling on the temporary setbacks and unfulfilled expectations of this life, fix your hope on the day when Jesus Himself will vindicate your faith and reward your efforts. Remember faithfulness—not success—is the hallmark of an effective ministry (1 Cor. 4:2).

Scripture Index

Topical Index

with the church. *See* Church
Immortality. *See* Eternal life

Jesus Christ
denying, 34-36
identifying with, 51-52
not being ashamed of. *See*
    Boldness

Kittelson, James M., boldness
    of Martin Luther, 77

Leadership, motivation of. *See*
    Motivation
Love
    affectionate, 23-24
    altruistic, 18-19
    supernatural, 47-49
Luther, Martin, boldness of, 77

Mercy, definition of, 19
Ministry
    effective, 79
    giftedness for. *See* Spiritual
      gifts
    sorrow of, 68-69
    success-oriented, 79
Mission, sense of, 11, 27
Motivation, principles of, 7-28

Not being ashamed of Christ.
    See Boldness

Onesiphorus, faithfulness of,
    75-76

Paul
    authority of, 15-18
    clear conscience of, 20-22
    compulsion of, 67-68
    duties of, 66-68
    forefathers of, 21-22
    hope of, 70-71, 79

    imminent death of, 9-10, 20-
      21, 70-71
    imprisonment of, 9-10, 20-21
    loving nature of, 23-24
    mission of, 11
    personality of, 30
    prayers of, 19-20, 2-23
    suffering of, 68-69
    See also Timothy
Peace, definition of, 19
Persecution. *See* Suffering
Peter
    his denial of Christ, 32-33
    his restoration by Christ, 33-
      34, 42
Power, God's. *See* God
Priorities, maintaining, 50-51,
    61

Resources in Christ, consider-
    ing our, 43-51
Resurrection. *See* Death,
    abolishing

Salvation
    author of, 55
    calling to. *See* Election
    security of, 66, 70-71
Scripture. *See* Doctrine
Security, of salvation. *See*
    Salvation
Self-discipline, 49-51, 60
Service, motivation for. *See*
    Motivation
Shadrach, Meshach, and Abed-
    nego, boldness of, 66, 78-
    79
Shame, avoiding. *See* Boldness
Spiritual gifts
    categories of, 38-39
    identifying your, 39-41
    receiving, 38
    renewing your, 37-41

uniqueness of, 38-39
using your, 40-41, 45
Spiritual growth, motivation
   for. *See* Motivation
Spurgeon, Charles Haddon, on
   holiness lightening our
   duties, 69
Steadfastness. *See* Trust
Success, godly perspective on,
   79
Suffering, accepting, 51-53, 60-
   61, 65-66

Timidity. *See* Resources in
   Christ
Timothy
   family of, 24-26

ministry of, 10, 31
motivation of, 7-28
problems of, 11-13, 30
spiritual gift of, 39-40
   See also Paul
Trials. *See* Suffering
Trust
   culmination of our, 70-71, 79
   object of our, 70
   result of our, 70
Truth. *See* Doctrine

Wisdom, applying, 49-50

Zeal. *See* Boldness

Moody Press, a ministry of the Moody Bible Institute, is designed for education, evangelization, and edification. If we may assist you in knowing more about Christ and the Christian life, please write us without obligation: Moody Press, c/o MLM, Chicago, Illinois 60610.